THIS D-I-Y JOURNAL BELONGS TO:

Piper O. Bell

[name]

THIS JOURNAL WAS BEGUN ON:

1, 26, 20

[date]

PS: If you are reading this book without my permission, BEWARE! Your nose hairs will grow at the rate of .5 inches for every minute of reading. If you keep reading, an hour from now, your nose hairs will be 30 inches long. You have been WARNED!

UNCLE JOHN'S D-I-Y JOURNAL: FOR INFOMANIACS ONLY

Copyright © 2015 Portable Press

Portable Press is an imprint of the Printers Row Publishing Group,
A Division of Readerlink Distribution Services, LLC.
"Bathroom Reader," "Portable Press," and "Bathroom Readers' Institute"
are registered trademarks of Readerlink Distribution Services, LLC.
All rights reserved.

For information, write: The Bathroom Readers' Institute,
P.O. Box 1117, Ashland, OR 97520
www.bathroomreader.com • e-mail: mail@bathroomreader.com

Cover design by Jen Keenan • Cover and interior illustration by Nick Halliday

The Bathroom Readers' Institute would like to thank the following people whose advice and assistance made this book possible:

Gordon Javna	Carly Schuna	Sydney Stanley
Kim T. Griswell	Hannah L. Bingham	Blake Mitchum
Trina Janssen	Melinda Allman	Rusty von Dyl
Brian Boone	Jennifer Magee	Aaron Guzman
Jay Newman	Peter Norton	Dwayne the Lab Rat

ISBN-13: 978-1-62686-430-6 • ISBN 10: 1-62686-430-6

Printed in the United States of America
First Printing
19 18 17 16 15 1 2 3 4 5

Uncle John's
D-I-Y JOURNAL
FOR INFOMANIACS ONLY!

By JOHN (That's me.)
& YOU (That's you!)

THE BATHROOM READERS' INSTITUTE

ASHLAND, OREGON

CAUTION: This book may be too tasty to leave where your dog can find it. If your dog does this (like my dog Porter did),

you will have to do this: Buy another Infomaniac's Journal and start again. (REPEAT AS NEEDED.)

John's GUIDE to INFORMATION DOMINATION

HERE'S A FACT: There's no point in sitting at your desk at school worrying about bloodsucking vampires. The biggest bloodsucker you'll ever meet is already inside your head. It's your br-r-r-rain!

That gray blob inside your skull sucks down about 20% of the blood circulating through your body. How do I know? Because I'm a self-diagnosed

INFOMANIAC*! I L-O-V-E information and I spend a lot of time (way too much, my mom says) finding out about...well, all kinds of stuff! If you're reading this, I regret to tell you, you're probably an infomaniac, too.

PLEASE TAKE THIS TEST.

For each question, circle "yes" or "no."

1. Do you want to know WHICH ants explode on contact? Yes / No

2. Do you care HOW astronauts manage to pee in space? Yes / No

3. Do you want to KNOW the U.S. government's emergency preparedness plan for a zombie invasion? Yes / No

4. Is your brain itching to start looking up answers instead of answering more questions? Yes / No

If you circled "yes" three or more times, you are definitely an infomaniac.

ONE MORE FACT: If you complete the D-I-Y pages in this journal you can join a super-select group of infomaniacs, founded by yours truly (that would be me, John). Just fill out the Certificate of Completion at the back of this book. Tear it out (or photocopy it) and mail it in! And I will send you an official membership card.

Go with the Flow!

John

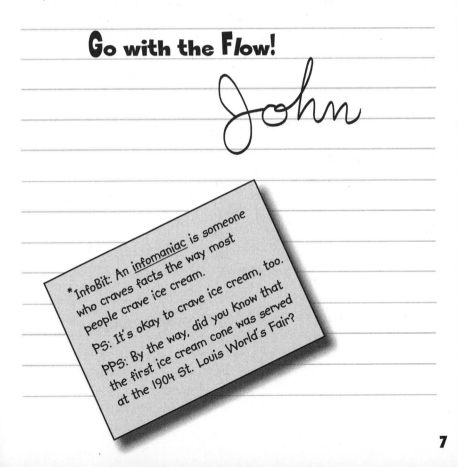

*InfoBit: An <u>infomaniac</u> is someone who craves facts the way most people crave ice cream.

PS: It's okay to crave ice cream, too.

PPS: By the way, did you know that the first ice cream cone was served at the 1904 St. Louis World's Fair?

This is me!

This is my dog Porter. He is my best friend, even though he drools...a lot!

This is Dwayne, the time-traveling lab rat. He popped out of my toilet one day to tell me about my future. Seems I will mastermind an Empire of Infomaniacs—Known as the Bathroom Readers' Institute—when I grow up.

Draw yourself!

Draw your animal best friend.

Draw a time-traveling animal. Write what it will tell you about your future.

Stuff About Me

1. I live in New Jersey. Here's a question: Why do they call it "the garden state"?

2. I have a plate with a plastic hot dog, plastic French fries, and a plastic pickle on my desk. Sometimes I forget that it's plastic and try to eat it.

3. I love MAD MAGAZINE (please do not tell my mom).

4. Garlic makes me break out in hives. (No. I am not a vampire. Please do not try to drive a ~~steak~~ stake through my heart.)

5. I am dyslexic.*

*InfoBit: <u>Dyslexic</u> means I had a tough time learning to read. It does NOT mean I'm not as smart as my brother, Mr. Bighead. It DOES mean I cannot be held responsible for spelling errors in this journal.

Stuff About You

1. I Live with my mom, dad and brother.

2. I LOVE FRUIT!

3.

4.

5.

6.

7.

NINCOMPOOP TEST

Sometimes my dad comes home griping about the people he works with. He tells me that I should make sure I never work with a bunch of NINCOMPOOPS. I have devised this test to detect nincompoops.

1. Have you ever stuck anything (besides toast) into a toaster to see what would happen? What? _No._

2. If you could release any kind of insect or animal in your school, what would you release? _Dogs & Cats. You could jus t pick one up dering class._

3. What was the best prank you ever played? _I thru water ballons at my brother and then pushed him in the pool! foly clothed!_

4. If you had to mix together two things that are in your refrigerator and eat them, what would you mix?

Red peppers with ketchup

5. Would you rather box against a kangaroo or a bear? *Kangaroo*

6. Would you rather wear a grass skirt and dance in front of your class or eat a live frog? *wear a grass skirt and dance in front of my class*

7. If you could meet any famous person, who would you pick? *Millie bobby brown*

8. Have you ever been tricked into doing something dumb? What and who tricked you?

9. Where do penguins live?

in the arktick

13

Flushers 'n' Gushers

Even though Dwayne the lab rat told me that I will grow up to be a trivia mastermind, I am considering other careers. Right now, INVENTOR is at the top of my list. These are my lists of the best and worst inventions.

CRAPPY

INVENTION: An alarm clock that wakes you up by rubbing your feet.
INVENTOR: Leonardo da Vinci

INVENTION: "Loudpaper"—a wallpaper stereo system.
INVENTOR: Alexis Mardas

INVENTION: The musical toothbrush. It played the Scottish ballad "Annie Laurie."
INVENTOR: Sir George Sitwell

INVENTION: The parachute overcoat.
INVENTOR: A tailor named Franz Reichelt. He jumped off the Eiffel Tower to see if it worked. It didn't. THE END.

GREAT

INVENTION: Pizza!
INVENTOR: Raffaele Esposito invented my favorite food in 1889, in Naples, Italy.

INVENTION: The chewing gum manufacturing machine
INVENTOR: Thomas Adams (in 1871). His company also invented Chiclets.

INVENTION: PEEPS (those marshmallowy Easter chicks)
INVENTOR: A Jewish guy named Sam Born.

INVENTION: Ear muffs
INVENTOR: 15-year-old Chester Greenfield. He got rich selling them during WWII.

Your Flushers

Invention:

Inventor:

Invention:

Inventor:

Your Gushers

Invention:

Inventor:

Invention:

Inventor:

Super-Dooper Plumbing Maze

"What happens to a lab rat when you flush it?" (See the end of this maze.)

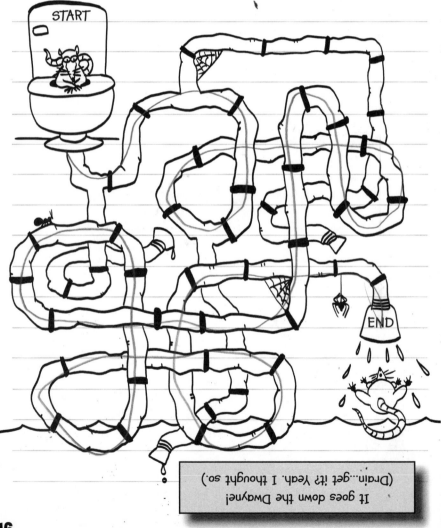

START

END

It goes down the Dwayne!
(Drain...get it? Yeah, I thought so.)

Your Plum**b**ing Maze

Your turn! START your maze with a riddle and END it with the riddle's answer.

Lunch Lady
Gets the Sack

Dear Lunch Lady,

You are required to attend a disciplinary hearing on May 14 at 2:30 p.m. The main items to be discussed at the hearing are as follows:
1. Feeding Pork to Muslim Students.

You should be aware that the disciplinary action taken could include termination of employment.

Sincerely,
The Principal

Write Back!

That letter was sent to a REAL lunch lady in England. And she was REALLY fired. Here's what she said: "I respect all of the children's beliefs, religions, and meal choices. This was just one mistake. I think firing me was really harsh."

Of course, there are two sides to every story. If you were the girl who found pork on her plate, what would you say to the lunch lady?

Dear Lunch Lady,

Sincerely,

*InfoBit: In England, to get the sack means to be fired from your job.

Invent-o-mat

My handy-dandy Invent-O-Mat (patent pending) is easy to use. Choose items from the list, stuff them into the top of the machine, and turn the crank.

nuts & bolts	snake skin	lightbulb
rubber bands	world map	wire
bent fork	screws	G.I. Joe head
rotten egg	gears	small motor
dirty sock	broken watch	empty soda can

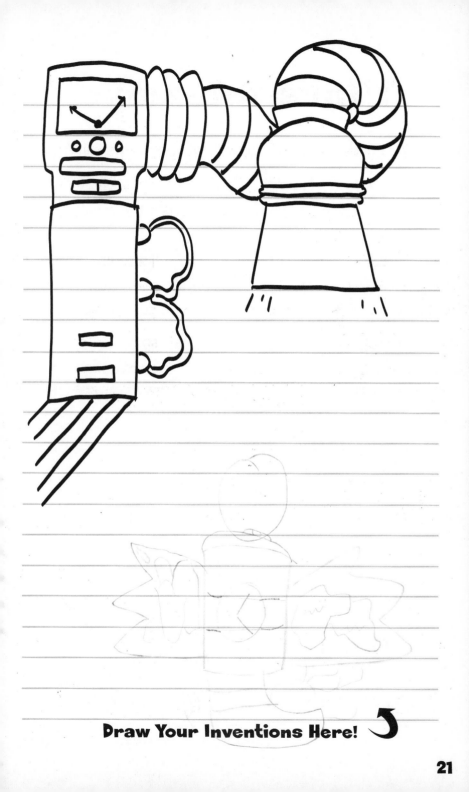

Draw Your Inventions Here!

That's Awesome!

Josh Casey of Madison, Wisconsin, has been a juggler for more than 20 years. He loves making people laugh and balancing things on...his face. The most amazing thing about Josh? He holds a Guinness World Record for sitting on whoopee cushions. Josh sat on 30 cushions (one after the other) in 30 seconds. That's one ph-f-f-ft! per second.

    I decided to write Josh a letter and ask him to draw himself doing something awesome. Check out what he drew!

WHEE!

Be Awesome!

Your turn! Draw yourself being awesome.

WARNING: If you do this awesome thing and it goes badly, the BRI cannot be held responsible.

Yo Mama!

26

D-I-Y Comic

Write and draw your own comic.

Underwear Stuff

One word always gets my teacher's attention: UNDERWEAR. Even if you say it under your breath, she hears it.

Miss Kawolski...this list is for you!

1. Washing your UNDERWEAR doesn't kill germs that live in your poop. It just spreads them to the next laundry load. (Eew!)

2. In San Francisco, it's illegal to use UNDERWEAR to wash or dry your car.

3. The astronauts aboard Gemini 7 flew home wearing nothing but(t) their long UNDERWEAR.

4. People in South America think wearing YELLOW UNDERWEAR is lucky.

5. A millionaire named Hetty Green said washing UNDERWEAR cost too much. So she NEVER washed her undies!

Your Undie Stuff

List the weirdest stories you know about UNDERWEAR.

1.

2.

3.

4.

5.

6.

Crazed Collectors

- These collectors were NUTZ! Russia's Peter the Great had a "kunstkammer." (That's a Chamber of Curiosities.) Guess what he kept inside? TEETH! How did he get the teeth? He pulled each one from the mouths of people he admired. (Ouch!)
- A Pennsylvania man collected 6,000 elephants (no...not live ones). One of them is an elephant POTTY CHAIR.
- A Philadelphia doctor collected medical oddities. The weirdest? The thorax* of John Wilkes Booth, the guy who assassinated ABE Lincoln.
- Dwayne the lab rat tells me my future self collects books, ukuleles, and (fake) severed heads.

*InfoBit: Thorax is another word for chest. The lungs and heart are inside it.

You Collect!

If you had a Chamber of Curiosities, what would YOU collect? Draw your stuff here.

Stuffed Animals

Ask an Expert

This morning, I had a question about a noise I'd been hearing. I tapped on the newspaper my dad hides behind at breakfast and asked him.

ME: Something is going "tap-tap-tap" inside my bedroom wall. What could it be?

DAD: How should I know? Ask your mother.

MOM: I have no idea, dear. Why don't you ask Grandpa John?

GRANDPA JOHN: What? Do I look like some kind of expert?

He didn't. So I asked Mr. Rat-o-Rooter, the guy who gets rid of pests in our building.

MR. RAT-O-ROOTER: Well, there's your red squirrels and your gray squirrels and your flyin' squirrels and your mice and your chipmunks. And your rats, of course. Dey all like to store food and build nests in da walls.

ME: So which one do you think it is, Mr. Rat-o-Rooter?

MR. RAT-O-ROOTER: Depends.

ME: On what?

MR. RAT-O-ROOTER: What time it is when you hear 'em. Mice, rats, and flyin' squirrels are nocturnal*. The rest of 'em are daytimers.

ME: I hear them at night.

MR. RAT-O-ROOTER: So...could be your mice or your rats or your flyin' squirrels.

ME: Uhmm.... So which one?

MR. RAT-O-ROOTER: What? Do I look like some kinda expert?

*InfoBit: <u>Nocturnal</u> means awake and active at night.

You Ask Experts

Your turn! Choose your five most pressing questions and find experts to answer them. (**WARNING:** Ask relatives at your own risk.)

YOU: How many teeth does a shark have

YOUR EXPERT:

YOU:

YOUR EXPERT:
name

YOU:

YOUR EXPERT:

name

YOU:

YOUR EXPERT:

name

YOU:

YOUR EXPERT:

name

Bug Body Parts

I've been thinking about becoming an entomologist. (That's a bug scientist.) Insects are super cool. They're kind of like aliens, with weird body parts that do unexpected things. A bug scientist named Roy Plotnick says insects have ears on every part of their bodies EXCEPT on their heads.

Here's an INFOMANIACS' TEST: Match each insect with its ear location.

INSECT	EAR LOCATION
Cricket	Knees
Tachinid fly	Thorax
Locust	Front legs
Katydid	Chin
Moth	Abdomen

More Body Parts

I like to think about why animals might need weird body parts. What do you think?

ONE REASON an octopus might need eight legs is to divide a big cake into eight perfectly equal portions. What are some other reasons?

ONE REASON a puffer fish might need spikes is to skewer some marshmallows for roasting. What are some other reasons?

ONE REASON a lobster might need gigantic claws is to crush and eat a walnut. What are some other reasons?

Holy Fish Scales!

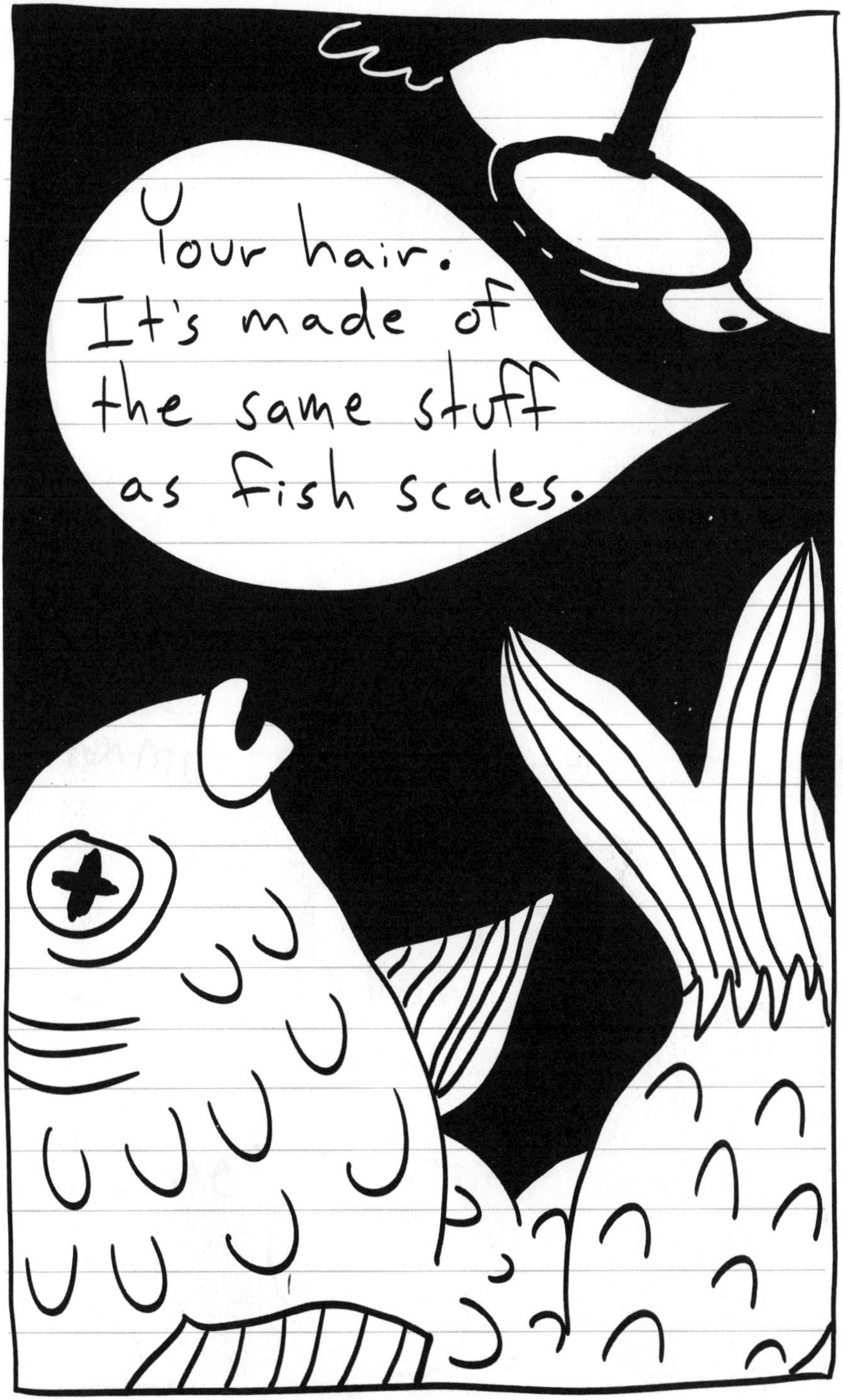
Your hair. It's made of the same stuff as fish scales.

Same stuff as reptile scales, fingernails, and feathers, too!
That's correct! How did you know?
Hmph! You're not Bradley Bighead's only Infomaniac.

Super-Colossal Fact Attack

The craziest facts I discovered this week:

1. A tiger's tongue is so rough it can lick the paint off a building.

2. The world's heaviest turkey weighed 86 lbs. and was the size of a German shepherd.

3. Albert Einstein's eyes are being kept in a safe in New York City.

4. The numbness when your foot goes to sleep has a name: obdormition.

5. One plop of elephant poop can feed and house 7,000 beetles.

6. Raw termites taste like pineapple. (If you decide to taste-test this fact, please note the results below.)

7. In the Netherlands, peanut butter is called pindakaas ("peanut cheese").

8. People who live in big cities have more ear wax.

9. Some monkeys in Thailand teach their babies to floss their teeth.

10. Alaska has more outhouses than any other U.S. state.

RAW TERMITE TASTE TEST
Do raw termites taste like pineapple? If you answered "no", please write what they taste like here:

Your Fact Attack

Create your own super-colossal fact list.

1.

2.

3.

4.

5.

6.

7.

8.

9.

10.

11.

12.

13.

Over the Moon

Q: When does the moon need to take out a loan?

A: When it's down to its last quarter.

I decided to collect moon jokes. But so far I've only found one. I filled the rest of the space with moon facts.

MOON FACT: The moon is freezing! And burning up! Temperatures on the moon's surface can span more than 500 degrees in a single day. In the middle of the day, it sometimes gets up to 250 degrees Fahrenheit. At night, it can drop down to -387 degrees.

MOON FACT: Mercury and Venus are the only "moonless" planets. Earth has just one moon, but both Saturn and Jupiter have more than 50. (Zoiks!)

moons

MOON FACT: Not all moons are round. Earth's moon is kind of egg-shaped. Some scientists say Hyperion, one of Saturn's moons, is shaped like a hamburger patty.

MOON FACT: There's no sound, weather, wind, or clouds on the moon. (Which would make the moon very boring if not for the next fact.)

MOON FACT: A 3-foot jump on Earth would carry you 18 feet, 9 inches, on the moon.

MOON FACT: The moon is moving away from the Earth at the rate of about 1/8 inch a year.

MOON FACT: President John F. Kennedy pushed for NASA to put a man on the moon. That happened in 1969. But the president's real wish was to send a man to MARS!

Moon Observer's Log

An hour after sunset every night for a week, go outside and look up at the sky.

Night 1

Date:

Draw the moon here.

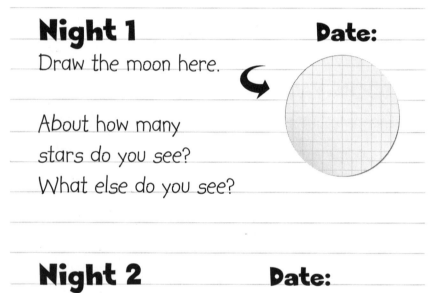

About how many stars do you see? What else do you see?

Night 2

Date:

Draw the moon here.

About how many stars do you see? What else do you see?

Night 3

Date:

Draw the moon here.

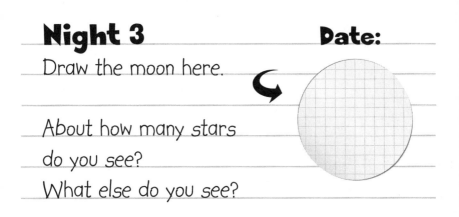

About how many stars
do you see?
What else do you see?

Night 4

Date:

Draw the moon here.

About how many stars
do you see?
What else do you see?

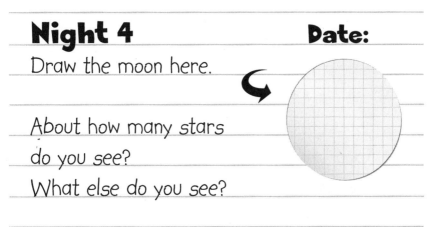

Night 5

Date:

Draw the moon here.

About how many stars
do you see?
What else do you see?

Night 6

Date:

Draw the moon here.

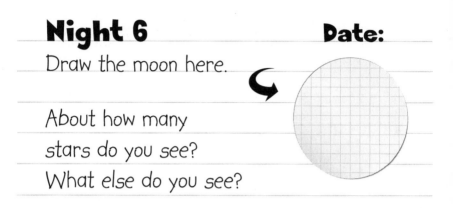

About how many
stars do you see?
What else do you see?

Night 7

Date:

Draw the moon here.

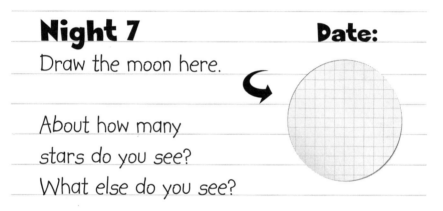

About how many
stars do you see?
What else do you see?

JoHn's JoKe Log

Q: Which is more useful, the Sun or the Moon?
A: The Moon, because the Sun only shines in the daytime when it's light anyway.

Your Moon Jokes

Collect your favorite moon jokes here.

Q:
A:

Q:
A:

Q:
A:

Q:
A:

Q:
A:

Q:
A:

Teacher Sayings

My teacher has all these weird sayings like, "Where there's smoke there's fire." Well, I'm here to tell you...that's not true. Every morning smoke comes out of our toaster. Why? Because Mom has burned the toast (again!). So far there hasn't been ANY fire.

I've been logging in Miss Kawolski's sayings all year and feel confident that none of them can be proven scientifically.

* It's always darkest before the dawn.
* A watched pot never boils.
* Two heads are better than one.
* Every cloud has a silver lining.
* Two's company, three's a crowd.
* Better late than never.
* The early bird catches the worm.
* An apple a day keeps the doctor away.

Mixed-up Sayings

Mix up the underlined endings from page 54
or make up your own.

It's always darkest _catches the worm_

A watched pot _A silver lining_

Two heads are _before the dawn_

Every cloud has _never_

Two's company, three's _keeps the doctor_
away

Better late than _never boils_

The early bird _a crowd_

An apple a day _better than one_

Toe-tle Jock

Why is it that infomaniacs are picked last for team sports? I don't get it. With my IQ, I should be picked first. Why? Strategy! Watching from the sidelines I can always tell which team is going to get creamed and why. But do team captains pick someone like me who can figure out a game plan? No. They do not.

    I used my research skills to find the perfect sport for my physique. It's (DRUM ROLL, PLEASE...) toe wrestling! The world championship happens every year in England. Wrestlers take off their shoes and socks and lock big toes. To win a match, you have to "pin" the other wrestler's toe for at least 3 seconds. Toe wrestling may become an Olympic sport, so I've been training. So far, I can do 10 dictionary lifts with my right big toe and 5 with my left.

Create a Sport

Who says you have to be a baseball or football player? Make up a sport at which you'd beat the socks off all the jocks!

Name your sport:

Tau along

Describe your sport:

List the rules:

1.

2.

3.

4.

My Future Empire

As you already know, Dwayne the lab rat traveled from the future to tell me that one day, I, John, an ordinary kid, will become the leader of a vast and tentacled trivia empire. Here is what I think it will look like.

Your Empire

You have (at least) two possible futures:
1. You will become a member of the BRI and spend your days researching oddities as one of my hyper-intelligent minions; or
2. You will create your own vast and tentacled empire. Draw your future here.

Down the Dwayne

Sometimes I like to draw comics. But...
I don't always finish them. (Note to
self: Find out if not finishing things is a
symptom of dyslexia.) Here's your chance
to become a comics-finishing genius. Fill in
the empty speech balloons and add your
own drawings to finish the story.

Cryptid Guide

There are zillions of living creatures on planet Earth, including some really weird ones. Some people (like my brother, Mr. Bighead) don't believe in **CRYPTIDs***. Personally, I don't care if cryptids are real. As part of my cryptid preparedness training, I put together this descriptive guide.

- **BIGFOOT:** This big, hairy, bipedal (two-footed) ape-man has been spotted in the Pacific Northwest. He's about 8 or 9 feet tall, and leaves behind 15-inch footprints. Bigfoot's cold-weather cousin, the Yeti, hangs out in the snow-covered mountains of Tibet and Nepal.

*InfoBit: A <u>cryptid</u> is a creature whose existence has not been proven (yet).

- **CHUPACABRA:** This cryptid has been spotted in South America. Some people say it has smooth skin. Others report reptilian skin or short, spiked, gray fur. It probably has fangs but might also have wings. Everyone agrees on one thing: the chupacabra sucks blood out of farm animals. I like chupacabra's nickname— "The Goat Sucker."

- **WHIRLING WUMPUS:** Have you ever seen Taz, the Tasmanian Devil from Looney Tunes cartoons? The wumpus looks like Taz except...it's 7 feet tall! It hides in forests.

When a logger comes along, it rears up on its powerful hind legs and spins so fast it becomes nearly invisible. The logger gets sucked into the whirling vortex, beaten to a pulp, and sprayed all over the surrounding vegetation. (Ugh!) Then the whirling wumpus spins to a stop and slurps up the goo.

- **MONGOLIAN DEATH WORM:** Never walk barefoot across the sands of Mongolia's Gobi Desert. Why not? Because you'll get footburn (ha!). Also, locals say a gigantic earthworm lives beneath the sand. They also say this monster worm can projectile-spit venom. If that's not scary enough, the

death worm is covered in slime
that can *kill* you with a single touch.

- **SNOW WASSET:** This cryptid
looks sort of like an otter, but
wa-a-a-ay bigger. In summer,
the snow wasset's fur is
green. It hibernates
(snoozes) through
the hot months.
After the first
snowfall, the snow
wasset wakes up...hungry. Its fur
turns white and it burrows into the
snow. For the rest of the winter
it prowls beneath the snow like a
submarine stalking ships. Why?
So It can sneak up on rabbits,
squirrels, voles, wolves, etc., and
gobble them down.

- **NANDI BEAR:** The forested mountains of eastern Africa are the supposed home of this supposed creature. Its name comes from  the Nandi people of Kenya. Nandi Bear been described as about four feet tall at the shoulders, with reddish-brown fur. Its forelegs are longer than its hind legs, making it look more like a hyena than a bear. The Nandi Bear eats only one thing: the brains of its victims (Oh, no! It's a zombie bear!). Sightings have been reported for hundreds of years. Some say it may be a surviving Pachycrocuta brevirostris, or "giant hyena." Those (supposedly) went extinct 500,000 years ago.

Your Cryptids

It's your turn! Describe and draw pictures of unbelievable (but possibly real) creatures you've seen or heard about.

Creature:

Description:

Draw your cryptid here.

Creature:

Description:

Draw your cryptid here.

Creature:

Description:

Draw your cryptid here.

Infomania Central

Dwayne the lab rat tells me that the future headquarters of my trivia empire is in Oregon. Hmmm.... Why would I locate the BRI in Oregon instead of New Jersey? Search me. But I have three theories.

1. Unlike New Jersey, Oregon actually LOOKs like a garden state.

2. Oregon has more ghost towns than any other state. (Who-oo-oo knew?)

3. Crater Lake, the deepest lake in the U.S., is in Oregon. It is 1,949 feet deep. How deep is that? If the Empire State Building were lowered into the lake, when it hit bottom, the top of the building's spire would be 500 feet below the lake's surface. Now THAT is DEEP!!!

Your Move!

Where will you live when you grow up? Choose what you like best at each level and follow the arrows to the next level. When you reach the end of the line, turn the page to find your future home.

Welcome to...

All interests lead to Oregon. No wonder I end there!

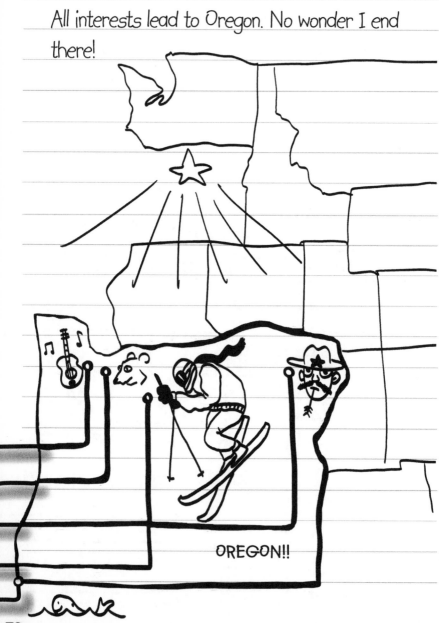

OREGON!!

Oregonia!

Don't like the results? Choose your favorite state and draw pictures to show why you'd rather live there.

Crime Watch

Thinking of a life of crime? BEWARE! Your own body parts leave behind evidence that can convict you in court. Personally, I have never considered a life of crime. (The cannoli I forgot to pay for at Beiderman's Deli does not count).

Why not? First: I'm an INFOmaniac, not a KLEPTOmaniac. Second: fingerprints! Fingerprints are unique—even if you're an identical twin. So are toe prints, footprints, palm prints, and even...tongue prints.

Police don't sweep crime scenes for tongue prints (yet). And there's no International Tongue Print Database (yet). But a team of Chinese scientists has already created 3-D scans of more than 100 people's tongues. So it's just a matter of time until your tongue can turn you in!

Your Tongue Print

My tongue print looks a bit like the biggest pyramid of Giza. My brother's looks like a clown's hat. What about yours? Now's the time to find out!

1. Dry your tongue by blotting it with a paper towel.

2. Pour a small amount of food coloring into a very shallow dish.

3. Press your tongue onto the dish, moving it back and forth to get food coloring onto all sides.

4. Press your tongue here.

2dO B4 I'm 2old

Yesterday, I asked Grandpa John why he has more hair growing out of his ears than on his head. "It's a sign of aging, Sonny Boy," he said. "By the way, have you seen my glasses?" (They were on his head.) "Or my teeth?" (They were in my milk glass...don't ask me why.) That's when I decided to make a list of things 2do before I get 2old to do them.

1. Brush my teeth after every meal so I don't end up losing them.

2. Give sage advise to a U.S. President.

3. See a moonbow at Yosemite's Falls.

4. Travel at the speed of sound.

5. Guard sea turtle eggs in Costa Rica.

6. Visit all seven continents.

7. Invent false teeth that can and MUST be kept in your mouth at all times.

Your 2do List

Grandpa John says getting old's not so bad. "The alternative is worse," he told me. "What do you mean?" I asked. "Croaking," he said. On that note, write your own 2DO BEFORE YOU CROAK list!

1.

2.

3.

4.

5.

6.

7.

Balancing Act

My teacher just announced the date
for this year's talent show. Super. My
biggest talent is putting my t-shirt on right
side out. Mom says that's not a talent.
It's a miracle. "You should be more like
Christian Stoinev, dear," she told me. "You
know. That nice young man we saw on TV
balancing on top of a pole on one hand?"

Right. Christian is a fifth-generation
acrobat. Acrobatics are in his DNA!
What's in my DNA (besides infomania)?
Channel surfing! Plus, he has a sidekick:
his Chihuahua, Scooby, who can walk on his
front paws. All my dog can do is nap.

Christian says developing a skill or
talent is all about not quitting. "Keep going
until you get it," he says. "It's not going to
come easy. If it did, everybody would do it.
You just have to go for it, no matter what!"

Practice Log

Most of us don't have Christian's hand balancing skills, but neither did he at age 10 when he first started. Choose a talent or skill to practice for a few minutes every day. Record your progress here!

Day 1:

Day 10:

Day 20:

Day 30:

Day 60:

Day 120:

The First Nerd

Most etymologists* agree that the word "nerd" was invented by Dr. Seuss. Yep. The green eggs and ham guy. He used "nerd" in his 1950 book *If I Ran the Zoo* to describe a weird-looking imaginary zoo animal. Before long, people started using the word to mean "a smart but socially awkward person." Nerd has also come to mean "a single-minded expert in a particular field."

*InfoBit: An <u>etymologist</u> studies the origins of words.

I'll probably be a nerd when I grow up, just like I am now. All I can say is,

it's better than being a "geek." Why? Because the original geeks were carnival performers who bit off the heads off live chickens. Think I'm kidding? Look it up!

Nerd Test

Uncover your nerditude. (If you dare!)

Color in ONE bubble for each question.

1. Which is higher?
- your weight
- your IQ
- your blood pressure

2. What is in your shirt pocket?
- a pocket calculator
- a lint-covered mint
- a detention slip

3. Which of these is NOT an element?
- Krypton
- neon
- snozzcomber

4. What's the grossest thing in your room?
- your dirty socks
- your Petri dish
- a dissected frog

5. Which is your favorite game?
- Mouse Trap
- Chess
- Twister

6. Which job would be more fun?
- rocket scientist
- BRI researcher
- English teacher

ARE YOU A NERD? If you are, you can figure it out from your answers. If you can't...well, there's your answer!

Magic or ...Murder?

Last night, my parents took me to see a magic show. It was awful! The magician sawed his assistant in half. Or at least, that's what I thought I saw. Dad said it was just an optical illusion. Here's what I saw:

1. The assistant stretched out in a box and the magician shackled her down.

2. He closed the box and sawed it in half.

3. She screamed. (I couldn't look.)

4. The magician pulled the box apart to show he'd really sawed her in half.

5. Then he pushed the box back together, took the blade out, and opened the box to reveal the assistant all in one piece without a drop of blood on her.

What the heck? I had to find out what was going on, so I did a bit of sleuthing. Turns out, as soon as the magician closes the box, the assistant wiggles out of the shackles and tucks her knees up to her chest. She stays that way while the magician saws the box in half and separates the halves. After the magician puts the box back together, she extends her legs and gets back into the shackles for the big reveal. **Ta-da!**

Harry Houdini's Escape Trick

1. While being tied up, make yourself as big as possible by inhaling and pushing your chest out.

2. Flex any muscles that are being tied up (Do it as subtly as possible so as not to raise suspicion).

3. Now relax. You'll get at least a half an inch of slack in the ropes, which may be enough to wiggle yourself loose.

How to Palm a Coin

My research into magic revealed one more magical secret: Here's how to palm a coin!

1. Open your hand and look at the coin. Touch your thumb to your pinkie finger. See the big fold in the middle of your hand? That's where you're going to store the coin.

2. Open your hand again and put the coin right in the middle of it.

3. Now flex the muscles in your palm, trying to grip the coin without making the rest of your hand look too weird. Can you keep the coin there and turn your hand over? Practice until you can!

Magic & Movies!

My best friend Marti Farti spotted the palmed coin the first time I showed her the trick. With friends like that, who needs enemies? (Sigh.)

What can you palm with no one noticing? Make a list here:

1.

2.

3.

4.

5.

Marti's favorite movie is *The Mad Magician*. It's a horror film from 1954. Marti is seriously warped. List your favorite movies:

1. frozen 2

2. Little shop of horrors

3. space balls

4. bob brady the internet

5. merry

That's Genius!

Miss Kawolski gave us a weird homework assignment for tonight (What else is new?). We're supposed to try to understand what makes someone a genius. I decided to see what real geniuses had to say about genius:

G. C. Lichtenberg: "Everyone is a genius at least once a year."

R. Buckminster Fuller: "Everyone is born a genius, but the process of living de-geniuses them."

George Bernard Shaw: "Few people think more than two or three times a year. I have made an international reputation for myself by thinking once or twice a week."

Federico Fellini: "Nietzsche claimed that his genius was in his nostrils, and I think that is a very excellent place for it to be."

Your Genius

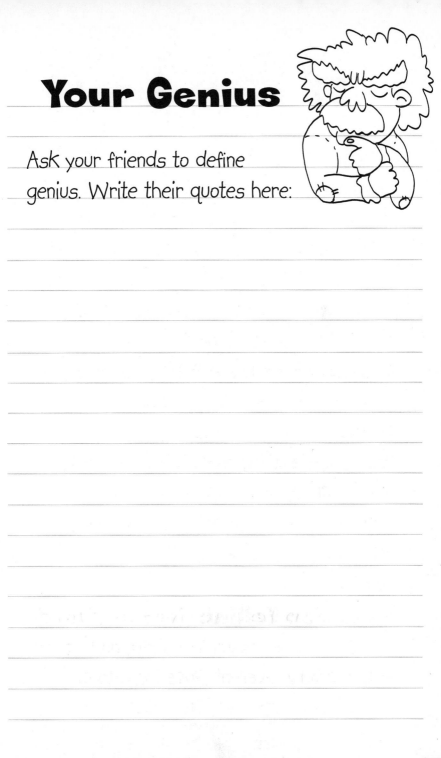

Ask your friends to define genius. Write their quotes here:

Dino-scarium!

When I was a kid—by which I mean, two years ago—I was obsessed with dinosaurs. I had more dino knowledge than most paleontologists*. Here are the three dinosaurs I would NOT want to meet:

SCARY—Pliosaur

Pliosaur was a water creature with a skull as long as a human man is tall. It had a total body length of more than 40 feet. Although pliosaurs mostly ate fish, some pliosaur skeletons have been discovered with dinosaur remains in their stomachs. What does that tell us? Pliosaurs ripped apart dinos that got close to the shoreline and had them for dinner as well. Paleontologist Richard Forrest says pliosaur was "probably the most fearsome predator that ever lived."

*InfoBit: A <u>paleontologist</u> is someone who studies animal and plant fossils.

SCARIER—Ankylosaur

Ankylosaur lived during the same time as T. rex, and whenever it was attacked, it made the predator's life as miserable as possible. In addition to being covered from head to toe in nature's toughest spikes and armor plates, the dino had a club as a tail. When whipped with enough force, the tail could gouge the skin of attackers and even crush their bones.

SCARIEST— Utahraptor

According to the Dinosaur Museum in Dorchester, England, Utahraptor wins the title of all-time "fiercest dinosaur." It may not have been as big or as strong as T. rex, but it had smarts on its side. Fingers and toes with foot-long claws don't hurt, either—that is, unless you're the prey.

Design-a-Raptor

In 2014, paleontologists digging in Venezuela discovered bones from a brand-new dinosaur, *Tachiraptor admirabilis*. Scientists think this raptor was about five feet long from nose to tail, that it had sharp teeth, and that it walked on two legs. It lived about 200 million years ago in a volcanically active region surrounded by valleys.

Based on that information, what do you think *Tachiraptor admirabilis* looked like? (Scales? Spikes? Feathers? A feather boa?)

What do you think it ate?
(Hint: Probably not doughnuts.)

Where might it have slept at night?

In a cave

How do you think it hunted and
defended itself from attacks?

Aint

defended.

Draw your raptor in the space below.

Get Greek'd

Socrates was this really smart guy who lived in ancient Greece between 469 and 399 B.C. (Apparently time went backward before the year A.D. 1.) Anyway, Socrates taught his students by asking lots and lots of questions. (They probably thought he was just being obnoxious, but actually probing questions help you learn to think more clearly and deeply about things.)
So, here are a few probing questions for all you potential infomaniacs!

What do you think is the most important thing you have done so far in life?

What makes you think that is true?

Sorry, I don't understand. Can you give me a few examples?

Is that all? What haven't you told me yet?

A Matter of Time

I spend a lot of time thinking about...time. Is the flow of time straight like an arrow? Or is it fluid like a river, as Albert Einstein thought? And how is it possible that if you take a set of identical twins and make one of them an astronaut, she will age less while traveling through space than her sister will while staying on Earth?

It's called "time dilation." Time passes more slowly for someone rocketing into space than for someone back home on Earth. That means, when the astronaut twin returns to Earth, she'll be younger than her sister.

How much younger? It depends. The faster and farther the astronaut flies, the older her twin when be when she gets home. The current record holder for space-time travel is Russian Cosmonaut Sergei Krikalev. He's spent more than two years in space. How far into the future has that put him? About 0.02 seconds—not even enough time to grab an extra cookie for the road.

Which twin would you rather be, the one that ends up younger or the one that ends up older?

younger

Why? *I actually do not real now Why I don't kind of do not care so I just picked one.*

If you could travel faster than the speed of light (186,000 miles in a second) and go backward in time, "when" would you go and what would you do?

Your Time Travels

Just because scientists haven't figured out how to time travel doesn't mean you can't plan ahead! Fill in the blanks with your time-travel plans:

If I could speed to any time in the past, I would visit the year _1968_ so that I could
see my mom & dad get
married and be older than me
with _none_ .

To change _____ ,
I would travel to the year_____. When I got there, I would _____

_____

_____

_____ .

The thing I regret most from my past is

_____

_____.

If I could travel back to that moment, I would

_____

instead of _____

_____.

If I could speed 25 years into the future, I
would go to _____,
so that I could _____

_____

_____.

If I could speed 100 years into the future, I
would go to _____
so that I could _____

_____

_____

_____.

Goofy Grownups

Lately I've been noticing that kids aren't the only ones who goof up on a regular basis. Grownups goof up, too. Here are some unbelievable (but real) goofs.

- Police in Connecticut arrested a man for robbery. When they asked him to return to the scene of the crime so witnesses could see him, the robber said, "How can they identify me? I had a mask on."

- A guy in London bought his girlfriend a $12,000 diamond engagement ring. He had a florist put it inside a helium balloon. The balloon (with the ring inside) was attached by a string to a bouquet of flowers. Right after he left the florist, the string slipped out of his hand and the balloon floated away.

Your Goofy Grownups

It's your turn! Log in goofs made by your parents or other grownups in your life. (Is this fun, or what?)

Shortz Tips!

I read somewhere that brains need exercise just like other parts of the body. One of my favorite ways to brain-train is to do crossword puzzles. Despite daily training, *The New York Times* puzzles still baffle me sometimes. I decided to ask crossword editor Will Shortz for some tips.

- **TIP 1**—Don't be afraid to guess.

- **TIP 2**—If you run into problems, erase and start over.

- **TIP 3**—If you're completely stuck, put the puzzle aside and come back later.

- **TIP 4**—Start with a Monday *NYTimes* puzzle (Mondays are the easiest).

- **TIP 5**—Always fill in an answer you are sure of first.

Once you get the hang of solving puzzles, try writing them. Here's a crisscross puzzle I just put together.

ACROSS

5. A witch's best subject in school.

6. What is a vampire's favorite fruit?

DOWN

1. Which goblin ate the Three Bears' porridge?

2. The undead.

3. An unusual Japanese monster.

4. After running a marathon, your feet are...

Be a Puzzler

Train for puzzle construction by building your first crossword puzzle here!

1. Fill in the answers. Make sure that all the letters you use make words while reading both across and down. Black out any squares that you haven't filled with letters.

2. Number your answers, making separate lists for Across and Down. The first Across answer is 1, and so is the first Down answer. Write each number in the square for the first letter of that answer.

3. Write clues for your answers. Give the clues (and another grid, with the numbers and black squares in it but no answers) to your mom and see if she can solve it.

anything

(Write your puzzle title on the line.)

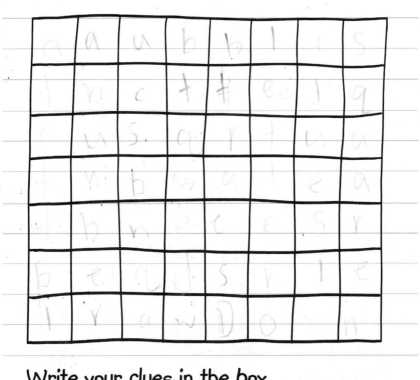

a	a	u	b	b	l	c	s
l	n	c	t	t	e	l	q
e	u	s	a	r	t	u	u
e	n	b	w	a	l	e	a
e	b	n	f	c	e	s	r
b	e	a	d	s	r	l	e
l	r	a	w	D	o	l	n

Write your clues in the box.

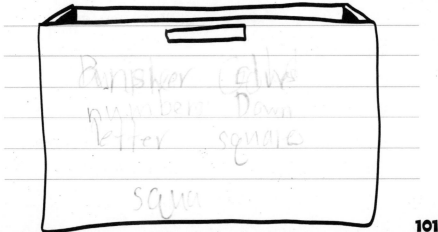

Answer   Letter
number   Down
letter   square

squa

Crisscross This

Want to try a few crisscross puzzles? All you need are words and clues. I've found puzzle-making to be easier if I choose a theme and come up with words to fit the theme. Use this theme list to get started.

PUZZLE THEMES

KINDS OF VEHICLES

SCARY THINGS

BOOK CHARACTERS

ANIMALS

SCHOOL STUFF

FOREST THINGS

MOVIE MONSTERS

FAIRYTALE STUFF

HEROES & VILLAINS

GAME CHARACTERS

THE UNIVERSE

GEMS & ROCKS

SPORTS TEAMS

STUFF IN MY PACK

REPTILES

MYTHICAL CREATURES

ENDANGERED ANIMALS

GROSS STUFF

Your Crisscross

OK. Here's some space. Choose a theme (or two) and create your own crisscross(es).

I'll Get (My Robot) Right on That

I spend a lot of time thinking about how to invent a ROBOT to do my homework for me. (I could probably get all of my homework DONE in the time I spend thinking about my homework-doing robot, but...it wouldn't be half as much fun.)

I've also been reading about robots (during homework time). Have you ever heard of Maillardet's automaton*? It was invented around 1810 by a Swiss watchmaker named Henri Maillardet. It was an early kind of robot that looked like the top half of a boy sitting behind a writing desk. The boy's upper body was welded into a machine filled with rotating disks. Believe it or not, the automaton could write in two languages: French and English.

Wondering how a machine could write? Those rotating disks worked sort of like a computer's read-only memory. They stored all the data needed for the robot to write—and even draw—in a creepily lifelike way. At the time Maillardet built his automaton, it had the largest memory of any mechanical device. Here is my version of one of the machine's drawings:

*InfoBit: An <u>AUTOMATON</u> is a mechanical device made to look like a human being. A predetermined set of coded instructions allows the machine to do whatever it is programmed to do.

Get Your 'Bot on It

Maillardet's humanoid automaton inspired a book titled *The Invention of Hugo Cabret* by Brian Selznick. The book was made into a movie. If you haven't read the book or watched the movie, what are you waiting for?

Now that you're back, draw your ideal robot here:

Make a list of things your robot would do for you (clean your room, receive kisses from your great-aunt, etc.):

1.

2.

3.

4.

5.

6.

7.

8.

9.

Mystery of the Disappearing TP

D-I-Y Mystery

Write and draw your own comic mystery.

?

Presidential Boo-boos

Last night I got into serious trouble with my Dad. What did I do? I'm keeping that to myself. But whatever it was, it wasn't nearly as bad as some of the things U.S. presidents have done. Check these out!

1. When Thomas Jefferson and John Adams visited William Shakespeare's childhood home in England, they cut wood chips out of one of the playwright's chairs to take home as souvenirs.

2. Until he found out it was healthier to swim with all his clothes on, John Quincy Adams skinny-dipped in the Potomac River every morning.

3. Warren G. Harding bet a priceless set of White House China on a poker game...and lost it!

Your Boo-boos

List your biggest
mistakes here.

WARNING: *This page is top secret! Anyone who reads this page without permission will immediately shrink to the size of a lab rat and grow ginormous teeth.*

MY #1 MISTAKE:

MY #2 MISTAKE:

MY #3 MISTAKE:

MY EXCUSES:

Future Cars

I'm not old enough to drive yet, but I know exactly what kind of car I want. It will:

* * fly,
* * drive itself, and
* * dispense ice cream sundaes.

Dwayne the time-traveling lab rat says there are cars in the future that actually do those things—well, except for the last one (but apparently there will be drive-thru ice cream shops, so that's just as good). By the year 2015 there will be cars that can

* fly at 125 miles per hour for more than 400 miles...without stopping for gas,
* detect hazards on the road,
* steer around turns, and
* park themselves.

Cars in Charge?

In the future, cars might be able to drive themselves. Here are a few questions to ~~think~~ *think* about:

1. If your car crashed, whose fault would it be? YOURs, or your car's?

2. Would your CAR need a driver's license?

no

3. Could police give a CAR a speeding ticket?

y

What questions can YOU think of?

1. *noir*

2. *none*

3. *none*

Your Future Car

What would your dream car look like?
Draw it here:

big, red, power ful

Check the things you'd like
your car to have:

- [ ] hot chocolate machine
- [x] video gaming device
- [x] crash-proof body
- [ ] ejector seats (for irritating riders)
- [x] voice-activated phone
- [ ] doggie door
- [ ] windshield video

Draw the car you think your favorite
superhero should be driving here:

Check the things your superhero's car
should have:

- [ ] x-ray vision windshield
- [ ] non-skid monster truck tires
- [ ] undentable exoskeleton
- [ ] ejector seats (for bad guys)
- [ ] voice-activated phone
- [✓] seat for sidekick
- [✓] tire-skidding glop sprayer

Oops!

I don't know about you, but I love spotting goofs, blunders, and bloopers in news stories.

GOOF: The *Oprington News Shopper* gave the names of three children as "Gavin, 3, and 11-year-old twins Helen and ugh." (Poor ugh!)

BLUNDER: After an earthquake struck Alaska's Aleutian Islands, a TV news anchor said it was "a 7.2 magniturd earthquake."

MAGNITURD

HEADLINE BLOOPER:
VOLUNTEERS SEARCH
FOR OLD CIVIL WAR PLANES

PROBLEM: The world's first military plane was the 1909 Wright Military Flyer. The Civil War ended in 1865. (Guess no one told the news writer!)

Oops Collection

It's your turn to collect oops, goofs, blunders, and bloopers. You'll find lots of them on the Internet and in newspapers.

GOOFs:

BLUNDERs:

BLOOPERs:

Ponder This!

When I grow up, I'll find experts to answer these questions. But for now, I'm just mulling them over. What do you think?

Why do cats' eyes shine in the dark?

Why do some people stick out their tongues when they're concentrating on something?

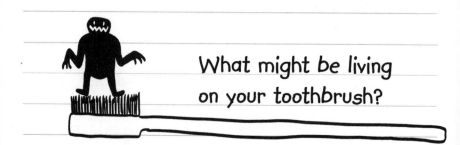

What might be living on your toothbrush?

How can you tell a girl earthworm from a boy earthworm?

Will I really get zits if I eat chocolate or fried foods?

Why do most kids hate liver and Brussels sprouts?

Why isn't our skin green or blue?

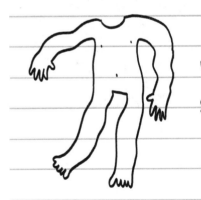

What's really in a hot dog? (And does anyone really want to know?)

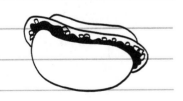

Worst Advice Ever!

Lately, everyone wants to give me advice: my brother–Mr. Bighead–my parents, my teacher, elderly relatives who call me "Sonny Boy" because they don't remember my name. Here's the stinkiest advice I've gotten so far.

ADVICE: "Boys don't play with dolls."
THE STINK: That one was from my big brother. I figured he knew what he was talking about, so I traded my collection of Star Wars action figures for some old, scratched-up Beatles records. Anyone still have a record turntable? I didn't think so.

ADVICE: "High school will be the best four years of your life, so enjoy it!"
THE STINK: It all goes downhill after age 18? That CAN'T be right!

ADVICE: "Respect your elders."

THE STINK: I get this one a lot. Grandpa John uses it as an excuse for everything.

ADVICE: "Keep your body in front of the ball and your glove on the ground!"

THE STINK: My baseball coach told me that was how to field a grounder. I did exactly what he told me and—guess what? The ball took an unexpected bounce and "Wham!" It hit me right in the nose. Thanks, Coach!

This Advice Stinks!

Write down the stinky advice people give you. Rate it on the smell scale, from garbage (stinky) to dirty diaper (stinkiest).

ADVICE:

ADVICE:

ADVICE:

ADVICE:

ADVICE:

Fear Facts

Everybody has fears, right? Alexander the Great conquered most of the known world in his time but that didn't stop him from being afraid of...cats! Yep—cats.

Every time I have to confront my biggest fears, I remind myself that Alexander was a scaredy-cat but that didn't stop him. Experts say fears serve a purpose: They help you survive. But over-the-top fears can get in your way. To help overcome my fears, I'm going to reveal my top three.

MY #1 FEAR? CATAGELOPHOBIA

(fear of being called "chicken," which is not the same as *alektorophobia*, fear of actual chickens) That wasn't so hard after all... unless someone actually reads this journal.

MY #2 FEAR? APIPHOBIA (fear of bees) If you're allergic, bee stings can make your skin swell up, make it hard to breathe, and even send you to the hospital. Okay...I admit it...I'm not allergic. So what am I afraid of? In a word: PAIN! That's normal, right?

MY #3 FEAR? LYGOPHOBIA (fear of the dark) There are plenty of good reasons for being scared of the dark. You can't see anything, so it's easy to trip and fall and hit your head and get a concussion and die. Really. It happens. Okay. Not that often.

My teacher says people who are afraid of the dark have over-active imaginations. Monsters in the closet, ghouls behind the door, gremlins under the bed...they're all just figments of my over-active imagination. Excuse me a sec. "HEY, MOM! Can I have a NIGHTLIGHT?"

Fear Face-offs

When I start to feel scared, I imagine face-offs between the things that scare me. For example, what would happen if the ghoul behind my bedroom door went up against a gigantic buzzing bee?

Beezilla vs. Ghoulashia

Battle Your Fears

Here's your chance. Name your fears, then draw them doing battle.

vs.

vs.

Animalia

In my quest to be the world's top trivia expert, I'm making a list of weird number facts about animals.

- The world's longest earthworms (found only in a small corner of Australia) can grow to as long as **12 feet** and as thick as a soda can.
- Squids have the largest eyes in nature: up to **10 inches** across.
- The longest flying-squirrel flight on record is **300 feet** (actually, they glide).
- By **age 15**, most tuna have swum more than a million miles.
- As a species, the platypus is **150 million** years old.
- A woodpecker's beak moves at a speed of **14–16 mph**.
- Alpaca wool comes in **22** natural colors.

Your Animalia

List away!

-
-
-
-
-
-
-
-

*InfoBit: <u>Animalia</u> is the group of living things that includes ALL ANIMALS.

Thud-ump...Thud-ump

What's so great about gym class? Sure, you get to do all kinds of things that are considered "inappropriate" in the classroom like kicking stuff, climbing on things, and using your "outdoor voice." But all that running around makes my heart pound.

I figured a brain-powered guy like me didn't really need gym class. Then I read this article in my mom's magazine about THE BRAIN-BOOSTING BENEFITS OF CARDIO. Wow! They are:

1. Clearer thinking

2. Better memory

3. Less stress

To get those benefits, I'll need to crank up my resting heart rate. But first, I have to figure out what it is!

Get a Pulse!

Trace a path down your thumb to where your palm meets your wrist. Place two fingers there. When you feel your heartbeat, count the number of beats for **15** seconds and multiply by **4**.

My resting heart rate is: _____.

My heart rate after...

   ...jogging in place for **30** seconds? _____

   ...doing **20** jumping jacks? _____

   ...dancing for **1** full song? _____

   ...walking around the block? _____

   ...standing on **1** leg for **1** minute? _____

What's next? You're an infomaniac! Do some research to find your ideal exercise heart rate and try to hit it.

Scrabble Babble

It doesn't take a genius to guess that I am a Scrabble pro. In fact, until I went up against my best friend, Marti Farti, I was Scrabble champion of B. A. Bighead Elementary. How'd she beat me? In a word—*syzygy**. But Marti still can't match my knowledge of Scrabble trivia. Can you?

1. Scrabble's original name was:
A. Lexico
B. Lotsa Letters
C. Wordgrams

*InfoBit: Syzygy [SIZ-i-jee] is an alignment of three celestial bodies.

2. The inventor of Scrabble was named:
A. Christopher Holmes
B. Alfred Butts
C. Tammy Nomenclature

3. There are _____ tiles in a
Scrabble game. (As long as you haven't
lost any.)

  A. 125

  B. 100

  C. 75

4. Scrabble is produced and sold in
_____ different languages.

  A. 29

  B. 46

  C. 12

5. At Scrabble tournaments, _____
is banned.

  A. Talking

  B. Loud sighing

  C. Suspicious behavior

Scrabble Words

Want to be a Scrabble champ? Start your word collection here. List words on the next page and use the point key below to tally up their point values. Then get ready to crush your opponents! (Example: BRAINIAC = 11 points)

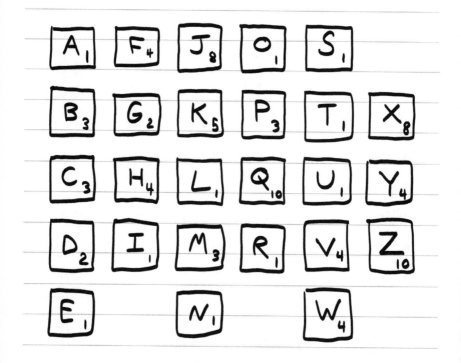

Word:	Points:
Word:	Points:
Word:	Points:
Word:	Points:
Word:	Points:
Word:	Points:
Word:	Points:
Word:	Points:
Word:	Points:
Word:	Points:
Word:	Points:
Word:	Points:
Word:	Points:
Word:	Points:
Word:	Points:
Word:	Points:
Word:	Points:
Word:	Points:
Word:	Points:
Word:	Points:

Tiger Trouble

Marti Trouble

HA! I've just proven that B.A. Bighead Elementary is home to at least one tiger. Draw what you think happens next.

WUTs Out There?

Ever since I watched the movie *War of the Worlds* I've been wondering if aliens are out there waiting to invade Earth. I don't know about you, but I think WUTs (Weird Unexplained Things) are definitely going on. Take Roswell, for example. What's Roswell? Read and learn!

WEATHER OR NOT: On July 4, 1947, a bright light shot across the sky over Roswell, New Mexico. It exploded and fell to earth on a ranch outside of town. Several men rushed to see what it was. What did they see? "An airplane without wings." They also saw three alien-looking bodies. Two were on the ground and one was visible through a hole in the side of the craft. Air Force officials issued a press release stating that a "flying disk" had crashed. But the next day...they asked for a "take back." It wasn't an alien ship after all, they said. It was...a weather balloon.

ALIEN TECH: In 1961, Colonel Philip Corso, of the U.S. Army Research and Development Department said, "Alien technology harvested from the infamous saucer crash in Roswell, New Mexico, led directly to the development of the integrated circuit chip, laser and fiber optic technologies, particle beams, electromagnetic propulsion systems, stealth capabilities, and many others. How do I know? I was in charge!"

APOLLO 14: Astronaut Edgar Mitchell said, "The evidence points to the fact that Roswell was a real incident and that an alien craft did crash. We all know that UFOs are real. All we need to ask is where do they come from, and what do they want?"

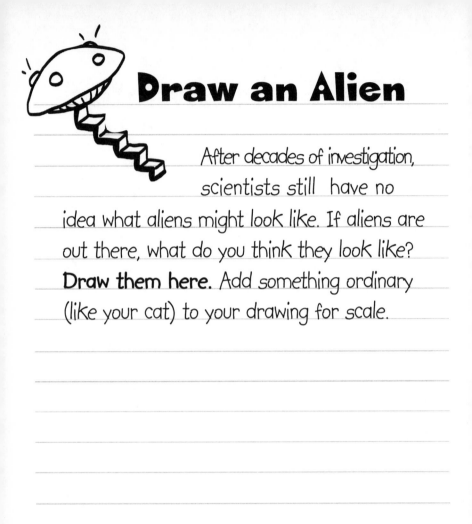

Draw an Alien

After decades of investigation, scientists still have no idea what aliens might look like. If aliens are out there, what do you think they look like? **Draw them here.** Add something ordinary (like your cat) to your drawing for scale.

UFOs Unscrambled

Before you tell your friends about that
UFO you saw make sure it's not—

_ _ _ _ _ (N V U S E),

A _ _ _ _ _ _ (T E M R O E),

RANDOM _ _ _ _ _ _ _

_ _ _ _ _ _ _ _ _,

(L G A N F I L P E C A S K J N U)

A _ _ _ _ _ (D O L U C),

OR A _ _ _ _ _ _

_ _ _ _ _ _ _ (T R A E H W E O N L A B O L), OR...

YOU'LL END UP FEELING _ _ _ _

(M U B D).

Fold-a-Hero

Let's say your brother advises you to get rid of your "dolls" (AKA Star Wars figures) and your buddies come over to play "hero smackdown." What can you do?

I had no idea, but my best friend, Marti Farti, learned to make origami puppets at summer camp. Hers were dressed in pretty kimonos, but I thought, "Hey! Those could be capes or leather jackets." So Marti taught me to make them.

STEP 1: Take a sheet of paper and lay it longwise or shortwise on a table or desk.

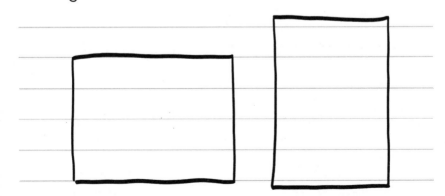

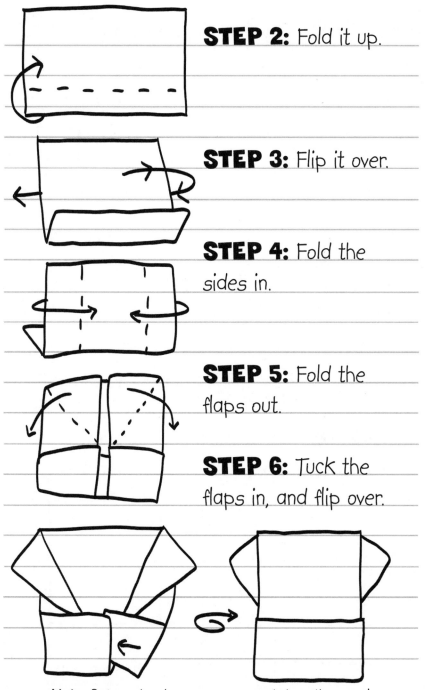

STEP 2: Fold it up.

STEP 3: Flip it over.

STEP 4: Fold the sides in.

STEP 5: Fold the flaps out.

STEP 6: Tuck the flaps in, and flip over.

Note: Before drawing on your puppet, turn the page!

Hero Faces

Before messing up a bunch of origami hero puppets, practice drawing costumes and faces here.

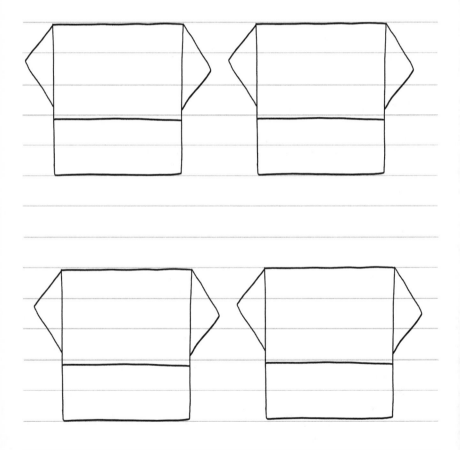

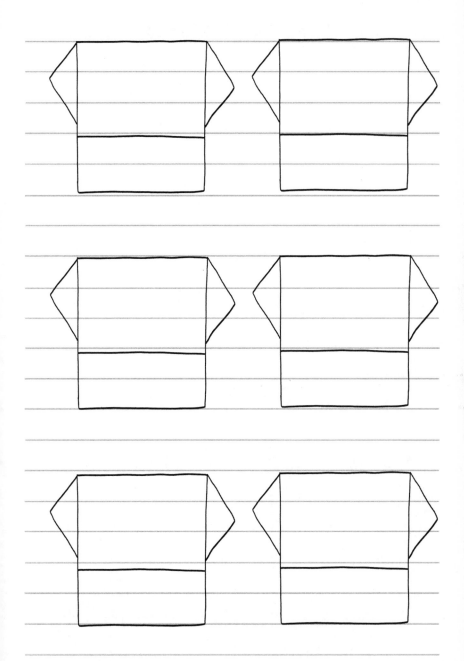

Songwriting 101

My band, Quacky Duck and His Barnyard Friends, hasn't had a top 10 hit yet. It's only a matter of time, of course, but I thought it might not hurt to get some tips from professionals. I asked a couple of songwriters for advice. Here are their tips:

FAKE IT. "I'm a big fan of 'close rhyme'—words that have similar sounds but don't actually rhyme like MINE and SLIDE, TEETH and SLEEP."—Anna Vogelzang

RHYME TIME. "Don't pick these words: Orange, silver, purple, month, and scalp. They have no perfect rhymes in the English language."—Anna again

EXAMINE YOUR HEAD. "Writing songs is a fun

way to think about all the stuff that goes on in your head. For me, it really feels like it's organizing my brain!"—Still Anna

JOURNALS (LIKE THIS ONE).
"Always carry a notebook when you're out so that you can jot down song ideas that occur while you're going about your daily business."—Debbie Poyser

CHANGE KEYS. "Make sure
your songs are not all in the same key. If you don't keep an eye on this your songs could all end up sounding similar to each other."—More Debbie

TAKE YOUR TIME! "There's one song
that I've been trying to write for fourteen years. Sometimes it comes all at once, and sometimes it evolves."—Rich Baumann (Fourteen years??? I'M not even that old!)

It's Your Song

Your turn to become a songwriter. Don't panic! Songwriter Jack Hardy once said, "The only thing that makes you a songwriter is writing songs."

Song Title:

Verse 1 (the part that tells a "story")

Chorus (the part that gets repeated after every verse)

Verse 2

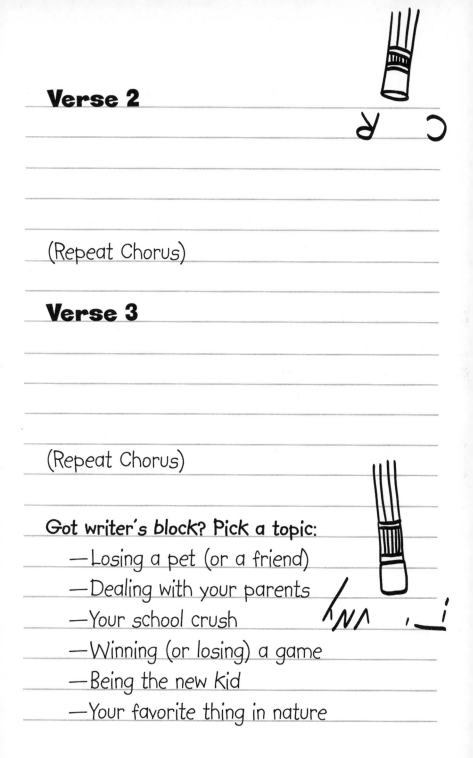

(Repeat Chorus)

Verse 3

(Repeat Chorus)

Got writer's block? Pick a topic:
- —Losing a pet (or a friend)
- —Dealing with your parents
- —Your school crush
- —Winning (or losing) a game
- —Being the new kid
- —Your favorite thing in nature

Draw Two!

Miss Kawolski gave us a worksheet about **homophones**, words that sound the same but mean different things. We're supposed to write examples, but I figured drawings would be even better. Want to help?

athlete's feat

athlete's feet

bored Kid

board Kid

bare legs

bear legs

"Hello, Dear!"

"Hello, deer!"

wild hair

wild hare

Free Fall!

I don't usually get questions wrong. So I was pretty sure I knew the answer when someone asked me this:

If you were standing at the top of a tall building and dropped a jar of mayonnaise AND a grain of rice at the same time, which would hit the ground first? Ignore air resistance.

The mayonnaise, right? That's what I thought. Boy was I wrong. Turns out that in free fall, with no air resistance, all dropped objects drop at the same rate. That means the grain of rice and the jar of mayo would hit the ground at the same time.

Why? Because without air resistance, gravity pulls everything toward Earth's center at the same speed: 9.8 meters per second every second. (That's called the acceleration of gravity.) The acceleration of gravity makes dropped objects speed up as they fall. The faster an object is moving when it ENDS its fall, the more energy and momentum it has. (Ever fallen off something at the playground? The higher you are when you start falling, the more it hurts when you hit the ground.)

Another way of thinking about it is that you actually weigh more upon impact when you fall from higher up. Don't believe me? Test it out on your bathroom scale. Stand on the scale to see how much you weigh normally, then take a little jump and watch the number change when you land.

Drop Zone

Now that you know a little bit more about acceleration, gravity, and free falling, watch them in action. Drop things from different heights and record the results here. Do the things you drop bounce back up? Land with a thud? Take a while to fall?

PS: Don't drop anything that will get you into trouble, or if you do, don't blame me!

Date:

What I Dropped:

What Happened:

PPS: Dropping a live frog on paper? Funny. Dropping one in real life. Not funny.

Date:

What I Dropped:

What Happened:

Date:

What I Dropped:

What Happened:

Date:

What I Dropped:

What Happened:

Facts from Uranus

I'm not making this list just because I think "facts from Uranus" sounds funny. Really. I'm not. (But...I'd better hide this from Mom. When it comes to Uranus, she has no sense of humor.)

1. Uranus is full of gas. Not the kind of gas you get from beans or the filling station down the street, but a special gas: helium. Helium makes birthday balloons float, zeppelins fly, and—believe it or not—it's what makes the Sun shine.

2. Each pole of Uranus is dark for 42 years at a time.

3. In 1781, astronomer William Herschel named this planet *Georgium Sidus,* after King George III of England. But

all of the other planets
were named after ancient gods,
so German astronomer J. E. Bode
renamed it after Ouranos, the Greek
god of the sky. The correct pronunciation is
not "your-anus." It's "urine-us." (Not much
better, is it?)

4. All of the giant outer planets in
our solar system have rings. Saturn has
23, Neptune has 9, Jupiter has 3, and
Uranus has 13 rings.

YOUR FACTS FROM URANUS:

1.

2.

3.

4.

Zombies Rule!

I've done a lot of research on world domination. Of all the things that could take over the planet, **ZOMBIES** are not high on the list (Most likely: space aliens or Asian beetles). So why does the U.S. government have a plan in place for a **ZOMBIE INVASION**?

The plan was created as a training exercise. It outlines a worst-case scenario involving a huge number of **ZOMBIES** eating and infecting a lot of people very quickly.

What kind of **ZOMBIES** could eat their way to world domination before anyone could stop them? Radiation Zombies (RZs), "Evil Magic" Zombies (EMZs), and my favorites...

DRAW A VEGETARIAN ZOMBIE.

Vegetarian Zombies:

VZs don't eat people. They devour plants. All of them. Until the whole planet is brown and plant-life-less.

Chicken Zombies: These

really exist! When hens quit laying eggs, farmers gas them with carbon monoxide and then pile them up to decompose. Some of the dead chickens come back to life, dig their way out of the pile, and stagger around for awhile. Then they drop dead again. Sad...

DRAW A CHICKEN ZOMBIE.

DRAW A SPACE ZOMBIE.

Space Zombies:

SZs are of extra-terrestrial origin, or can be caused by ET-radiation or toxins.

165

You Rule the World

Actually, I plan to rule the world myself. But in case I don't succeed, give it your best shot! The last pages of the *Infomaniac's Do-It-Yourself Journal* are for you to record your plan for WORLD DOMINATION.

HERE ARE THE RULES:

1. Include all the important things that happen in your life on the way to WORLD DOMINATION.

2. Draw comics to show how you went from being an INFOMANIACAL KID to RULER OF THE WORLD.

3. HAVE FUN!!!!

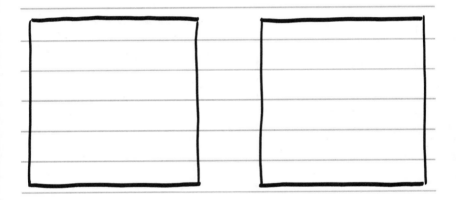

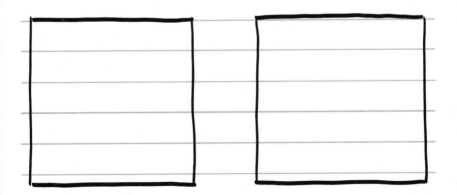

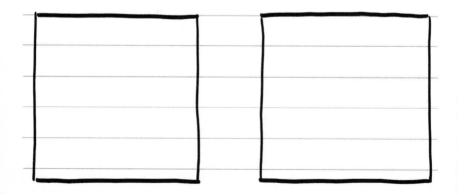

CERTIFICATE OF COMPLETION

I _____,
[name]

HEREBY CERTIFY THAT I COMPLETED
THE INFOMANIAC'S D-I-Y
JOURNAL FOR BOYS ONLY
ON

_____.
[date]

Tear out (or photocopy) this page and mail it to: BRI, P.O. Box 1117, Ashland, Oregon, 97520. You'll receive a free BRI membership card, discounts when ordering directly through the BRI, and a permanent spot on the BRI honor roll!